SYNDROMEDY

The Totally Unofficial Field Guide to Weird Human Behavior

by Jamison Carrier
with Dr. Sy Camore

Foreword

By Amy Figment

Introduction

Diagnosing the Slightly Off

PART I: Social & Digital Anxiety

The Modern Emotional Battlefield

1. **Involuntary Laughter Tagging Disorder (ILTD)**
   You're not fine. You're just buffering with "lol."
2. **Group Text Aversion Disorder (GTAD)**
   You were added without consent. You will never recover.
3. **LinkedIn Validation Disorder (LVD)**
   Because nothing says "career confidence" like desperately tracking post views.

4. **Menu Decision Paralysis (MDP)**
   You knew you were going out. Why are you still panicking?
5. **Emotional Soft Launching Syndrome (ESLS)**
   All feelings must be disguised as memes, song lyrics, or "haha kinda true."

PART II: Domestic Dysfunction

Because You Definitely Married Someone with Opposite Settings

6. **Situational Object Blindness Disorder (SOBD)**
   "Where's the Ranch?" It's in front of your face, Jeremy.
7. **Default No Disorder (DND)**
   If joy is suggested, your instinct is to block it.
8. **Checklist Addiction Syndrome (CAS)**
   You wrote it down just to check it off. Again.
9. **Compulsive Vacation Itinerary Syndrome (CVIS)**
   We can rest when we die.
10. **Amazon Box Blindness (ABB)**
    You bought it. You forgot it. It's in the laundry room.

PART III: Fitness Delusion & Performance Theater

Where Self-Improvement Meets Vanity in Moisture-Wicking Fabric

PART IV: Career & Corporate Chaos

Where Everyone's a Brand and No One's Okay

> *You can't not fix things. Even passive-*
> *aggressively.*

20. **Chronic One-Upper Syndrome (COUS)**
    Oh, you did something cool? They've done it
    better. In Europe. Twice.

PART V: Sports Psychosis & Suburban Glory

"They're 8 years old. No, they're not going pro."

21. **Vicarious Athlete Syndrome (VAS)**
    You peaked in high school. Now your kid has to
    avenge your JV career.
22. **Armchair Ref Rage Disorder (ARRD)**
    You saw the whole play from 83 feet away. The
    umpire? Blinded by bias.
23. **Team Identification Delusion (TID)**
    "We need to win this week." Sir, you sell
    insurance.
24. **Fantasy Football Identity Crisis (FFIC)**
    You lost sleep over a tight end who doesn't know
    you exist.

Bonus Chapter: Technological Mismatch Disorder

They changed the Wi-Fi name and now I can't watch
church.

Final Chapter: Yes, It's a Thing.

A closing message of grace, humor, and shared weirdness. You're not broken. You're just funny. And definitely diagnosable.

A Note from the Author

In Case You Thought This Was Just About Laughing

About the Author

Real Jamison. No clipboard.

Co-Conspirators

Because none of this dysfunction happened in isolation.

Jamison Carrier

Foreword

by Someone Who Has Absolutely No Business Writing a Foreword

Hi. My name is Amy, and I once cried in a parking lot because someone heart-reacted to my text instead of replying with words.

I wasn't always like this.

Okay, that's a lie—I was always like this. I just used to think I was "quirky" or "empathetic" or "just really in tune with social dynamics."
Turns out, I was simply marinating in low-grade chaos and calling it *a personality*.

Enter **Dr. Sy Camore** (pronounced CAY-more, like *say more*, but you can do that later).

I met Dr. Camore after a particularly bad week.

I had RSVP'd "maybe" to six different baby showers because I didn't want to commit.
I'd accidentally wrote "lol" in a sympathy card.
And I'd spent 37 minutes deciding between two types of hummus before abandoning the grocery store altogether.

I was unraveling.

And this man—this calm, unblinking therapist in a pinstripe suit with clear glasses and emotionally exhausted eyes – holding a clipboard like it contained your entire personality – just looked at me and said:

"You may be suffering from Mild Decision Trauma, exacerbated by internalized snack shame and a full-blown case of Passive-Aggressivitis."

He didn't even blink.

That moment changed my life.

Because I realized something powerful:
We are all one group text, one vague Instagram quote, or one silent "Read at 10:42 AM" away from completely losing it.

This book? It's not really about disorders in the medical sense.
It's a mirror.
A beautifully distorted, laugh-out-loud, *"oh no that's definitely me"* mirror.

Dr. Camore has compiled a deeply unprofessional—but alarmingly accurate—field guide to the psychological micro-scratches we all carry.
It's part therapy, part roast, and 100% *"Oh man, I thought I was the only one."*

You'll laugh.
You'll cringe.
You'll text someone mid-chapter to say, "This is so you," while secretly knowing it's actually you.

And maybe—just maybe—you'll come away with a little more grace for your weirdness.
Or at least learn how to stop using 14 exclamation marks in professional emails.

Jamison Carrier

So welcome, dear reader.
You're not broken.
You're just... hilariously human.

And Dr. Camore is ready to diagnose you with
something that doesn't exist—
but definitely feels real.

Now turn the page.
Therapy starts now.

lol.

— Amy Figment
Recovering Overthinker, One-Time Emotional
Support Friend, Still Typing "let me know if that
makes sense" in emails to explain basic thoughts.

Syndromedy

Jamison Carrier

Introduction

Diagnosing the Slightly Off

Yes, you have a syndrome.
You just haven't been diagnosed yet.

You're not alone.
You're not broken.
You're just a little off—and that's okay.

In fact, your off-ness might be what makes you loveable. And predictable. And completely exhausting to travel with.

This book is a satirical field guide to the syndromes we all carry—the irrational behaviors, emotional landmines, and endearing little meltdowns that make us who we are. You won't find these in the Diagnostic and Statistical Manual of Mental Disorders (DSM). You'll find them in group texts, checkout lines, team meetings, and family vacations.

Each chapter is a case file.
Each disorder is fake—but also painfully real.
Each patient? Loosely based on *you*. Sorry about that.

These are not clinical diagnoses.
These are... observations.
From a totally unlicensed, emotionally overworked therapist named **Dr. Sy Camore.**
He's not board certified, but he *does* own a

clipboard and occasionally sighs deeply before saying things like, "Ah, yes. Classic Default No Disorder."

Syndromedy is meant to make you laugh—mostly at yourself. But it's also an invitation to notice the strange little glitches in others… and love them anyway. That person who narrates their workout to everyone in line at Starbucks? Diagnosable. The one who can't RSVP without spiraling? Definitely diagnosable. The guy who ghosted a group text like it owed him money? He's featured in Chapter Two.

So, settle in.
Breathe deeply.
Take notes if you must.
And remember:

You're not broken.
You're just funny.
And definitely diagnosable.

Jamison Carrier

PART I: Social & Digital Anxiety

The Modern Emotional Battlefield

Chapter One

Involuntary Laughter Tagging Disorder (ILTD)

"I'm not actually laughing. I'm just scared of sounding serious."

Patient: Lauren P.
Age: 27
Occupation: LOL Distributor / Emotional Softener / Human Emoji
Referral Source: Her best friend, who received a 3-paragraph breakup rant ending in "lol."

Session Notes:

Lauren communicates primarily through text. Every sentence is followed by "lol," or "hahahaha" like emotional punctuation.

When I asked how she was doing, she replied:

"Honestly not great lol."

She has been known to send the following:

- "I think I'm depressed lol"
- "Just got ghosted again haha it's fine"
- "I'm dead lol" *(She was very much alive.)*

Classic ILTD.

Symptoms Include:

- Appends "lol" to anything remotely vulnerable
- Replaces periods with "hahaha" to soften emotional impact
- Cannot end a text without signaling "I'm not mad" or "please don't think I'm intense"
- Has not expressed a raw emotion in text form since 2013

When asked why she does it, Lauren replied:

"I just don't want people to think I'm, like…
serious serious, you know?"
Then added:
"lol"

Notable Behavior:

Lauren once confronted a cheating ex with:

"Hey, I know you lied to me lol but it's whatever haha no worries :)"

She later admitted she was "sobbing while typing."
But the "lol" was for protection.

Therapist's Interpretation:

Involuntary Laughter Tagging Disorder is a digital self-defense mechanism—

a way to sound chill while experiencing deep emotional combustion.

The "lol" is not laughter.
It's a buffer.
A shield.
A neon sign that says: *"Please don't reject me for being intense."*

Treatment Plan:

1. **The Honest Text Challenge:**
   One message per day with no emotional qualifiers.
   (Lauren broke into hives.)
2. **Punctuation Rehab:**
   Use periods without "lol" for 24 hours.
   (She described this as "psychological nudity.")
3. **Affirmation Rewriting:**
   Turn "I'm sad lol" into "I'm sad. And that's okay."
   (She added: "This feels aggressive.")
4. **Therapy Phrase of the Week:**

   "I can be honest without apologizing for it."

SELF-ASSESSMENT: ILTD

"I'm fine lol" — A Collection of Emotional Lies

1. Your friend says: "I'm tired of being the only one who tries." You respond with:
A. "That sucks. I hear you."
B. "I feel the same way."

C. "Omg same lol"

D. "Bahahaha right?? We're so broken hahaha"

2. You want to say: "I'm upset." What actually comes out?

A. "I'm upset."

B. "I'm kinda bummed."

C. "I'm fine lol"

D. "Haha it's chill, I'm just dying inside lololol"

3. You've ended a serious conversation with:

A. A heart emoji

B. A period

C. "Lol"

D. "Hahahaha anywayyy"

Mostly C's or D's?

You're emotionally soft-launching your feelings.

You've got ILTD.

We see you.

We hear you.

And we're not laughing. *(But like… in a good way.)*

Doctor's Notes:

Lauren is now limiting herself to one "lol" per message.

She relapsed yesterday after a parking ticket.

We forgave her.

Because, life's hard. Lol

Syndromedy

CHAPTER TWO

Group Text Aversion Disorder (GTAD)

"You were added without consent. You will never recover."

Patient: Blake R.
Age: 35
Occupation: Operations Manager / Text Thread Escape Artist
Referral Source: His wife, who added him to the neighborhood babysitting co-op group text and then had to explain why he left it 47 seconds later.

Session Notes:

Blake entered the session twitching. Not physically. Digitally.
He'd just been re-added to a group thread he had tried—unsuccessfully—to leave twice.

He scrolled through a week's worth of messages and showed me his screen:

- "Hey y'all, do we have a soccer game Thursday?"
- "Yes, it's at 6. Wear the white jerseys!!"
- "Wait, are we bringing snacks?"
- "Emily has oranges. We still need napkins."
- "Can someone bring extra chairs?"

Blake whispered, "I don't even have a kid named Emily."

Then he showed me his battery usage report. Text Messaging was consuming **38%** of his phone's power.

He said, "I don't *read* these threads. I just *live* in fear of them."

Classic GTAD.

Symptoms Include:

- Visceral dread when the words *"You've been added"* appear
- Turning off notifications, then checking compulsively anyway
- Accidentally offending people by "leaving the conversation"
- Feeling physically trapped in a digital hostage situation
- Audibly groaning when the thread name includes emojis

Notable Incident:

Blake was once added to a bachelor party group text titled "Vegas Bros"
He didn't know the groom.
He was invited because someone mistook him for another Blake.
He muted the thread, said nothing, and received 91 messages in 36 hours.

Topics included:

- Matching outfits

Jamison Carrier
- Axe-throwing reservations
- Who's bringing the "special deck of cards"

He still has no idea what that last one meant.
But he wakes up at night thinking about it.

Therapist's Interpretation:

Group Text Aversion Disorder isn't about communication.
It's about **chaotic overload** disguised as social engagement.

People with GTAD tend to be:

- Highly structured
- Conflict-avoidant
- Emotionally allergic to "typing bubbles"

To Blake, a group text is not a helpful coordination tool.
It's an unfiltered chaos stream that he didn't ask for and can't escape.

Treatment Plan:

1. **Thread Triaging:**
   Respond only to direct questions.
   Ignore side chatter unless tagged by name *twice*.
2. **Boundary Phrasing Practice:**
   Learn phrases like:

"Hey, I'm stepping out of this thread—feel free
to loop me in directly if needed!"
(Say it once. Then mute.)

3. **One-Thread Rule:**
   No more than one active group thread at
   a time.
   He must choose between work, family, or
   "GroomSquad24".
4. **Therapy Phrase of the Week:**

"I am not obligated to follow a conversation
about juice boxes for children I didn't create."

Self-Assessment: Do You Have GTAD?

"You left the chat." Yes. Proudly.

1. A new thread starts. Your first reaction is:
   A. "Yay! Connection!"
   B. "Okay, let's coordinate."
   C. "Who added me?"
   D. *Leaves thread immediately and denies all
   knowledge.*
2. You receive 12 unread messages. You:
   A. Read them all.
   B. Skim for relevance.
   C. Panic-scroll.
   D. Delete the thread and consider
   changing your number.
3. You're tagged in a message about snacks
   for the team. You reply:
   A. "I'll bring goldfish crackers!"
   B. "Let me check."
   C. "Do we really need snacks?"

D. "I'm in Canada that weekend." *(You are not.)*

4. The group changes its name to "Blake's Birthday Bash." You:
    A. Feel honored
    B. Feel pressure
    C. Feel rage
    D. Block the sender

Mostly C's or D's?

You've got GTAD.
And you're not alone—well, unless you want to be.

Doctor's Notes:

Blake is making progress. He now responds to group messages with a simple "Noted."
He's also experimenting with the "custom mute" feature.
Next week, we're working up the courage to be added to a fantasy football thread.
Prayers appreciated.

Syndromedy

Chapter Three

LinkedIn Validation Dependency (LVD)

"If I don't get at least 47 'congrats!', did I even post anything?"

Patient: Chad H.
Age: 39
Occupation: Business Development / Title Inflator / Connection Collector
Referral Source: His wife, after he referred to a LinkedIn post as "one of the most vulnerable things I've ever shared."

Session Notes:

Chad opened the session by saying:

"Sorry, I might be a little distracted—I've got a post trending."

He then showed me his phone.

It was a *"Today's my last day..."* post—complete with a black-and-white photo of an empty desk and a caption that included the words *grateful, bittersweet,* and *new chapter.*

The post had 62 reactions and 17 comments. He'd replied to each one individually. With tailored emojis.

Classic LVD.

Symptoms of LVD:

- Refers to job transitions as "career evolutions"
- Posts inspirational quotes on Tuesdays with no context
- Has "connector, disruptor, visionary" in his headline
- Says things like:

> "Let's connect!"
> "This one's for the community."
> "Feeling seen by these metrics!"

Chad's profile picture is him in a blazer, laughing at something just off-camera.
His bio includes the line:

"I believe in people, progress, and putting pineapple on pizza."

He thinks this makes him relatable.

Notable Incident:

Chad once got upset that a colleague didn't comment on his promotion announcement.
He confronted them via Slack.

The colleague said:

"I liked it. Isn't that enough?"

Jamison Carrier

Chad replied:

"Engagement drives engagement, man. We rise together."

He was not kidding.

Therapist's Interpretation:

LinkedIn Validation Dependency is not about ambition.
It's not even about connection.

It's about curated identity management—an algorithmic addiction to affirmation.

Chad isn't climbing the corporate ladder.
He's building a personal brand—one #LeadershipMatters post at a time.

He doesn't just want to succeed.
He wants to succeed *publicly*.
And get 37 clapping emojis in the comments to prove it.

Recent Behavior:

Chad wrote a post about leaving a job he was fired from, and described it as:

"A chance to pause, realign, and embrace what's next."

He ended it with:

"If you've ever faced a setback that led to growth, I see you. We are not alone. #Resilience #Gratitude #GrowthMindset"

He got 89 reactions and three DMs offering contract work.
He called it *"a win for authenticity."*

Treatment Plan:

1. **Content Detox**
   No posts for one week. Not even to celebrate someone else's milestone.
   (Chad created a draft folder for emergencies. It has 27 posts in it.)
2. **Engagement Limiting**
   Max: 3 emoji reactions per day.
   Comments must include real words.
   No "Let's gooo!" or "Love this for you!"
3. **Phrase Reduction**
   Remove buzzwords using a shock collar system.
   Words like *synergy*, *disruption*, and *growth journey* now trigger mild discomfort.
4. **Mirror Therapy**
   Look into the mirror and say:

   > "I am more than my profile."
   > "I can achieve things without announcing them."
   > "No one knows what a thought leader is."

5. **Phrase of the Week**

Jamison Carrier

> "My worth is not measured in
> likes from strangers named
> Brent."

Self-Assessment: LVD

*"I don't know what this job is, but I sure know what it
looks like."*

1. How many emojis do you typically use in a single LinkedIn comment?
A. 0–1
B. 2–3
C. 4+ (must include fire and clapping)
D. I rotate them seasonally for maximum impact

2. When someone announces a new job, you:
A. Wish them well
B. Hit "Like"
C. Comment with "So proud of you!" despite not knowing them
D. Screenshot it to compare your own post performance

3. You updated your headline to include:
A. Your job title
B. A mildly creative descriptor
C. "Coach | Connector | Culture-Driven Collaborator"
D. "Humaning my way through the professional space"

4. You describe LinkedIn as:
A. A networking tool
B. A digital resume
C. A platform for authentic storytelling

D. "Where I go to be the best version of myself... publicly."

Mostly C's or D's?
You may have LVD.
Put the phone down.
Your post will still happen—even if you don't hashtag it.

Doctor's Notes:

Chad is progressing slowly.
He now waits 30 minutes before posting a job update.
He's considering changing his profile pic to something without a laughing face.

We're cautiously optimistic.
But if he says *"crushing Q2"* one more time, we're sending him back to Facebook.

Chapter Four

Menu Decision Paralysis (MDP)

"One menu. Infinite regret."

Patient: Brittany S.
Age: 28
Occupation: Lifestyle Blogger / Indecision Engine
Referral Source: Her boyfriend, who is "tired of pretending he doesn't care what she orders."

Session Notes:

Brittany arrived 17 minutes late.
Her reason?

"I stopped to get a smoothie but... I couldn't decide on a base. Or a milk. Or a size. So I panicked and got gas instead."

I offered her water.
She asked:

"Still or sparkling?"

I asked if she wanted to start by talking about her week.
She said:

"Ugh. Should we start there? Or maybe childhood? Or... actually, you pick."

This is classic MDP behavior:

- Fear of making the wrong choice
- Deep distrust in one's own preferences
- A belief that every decision, no matter how small, will be judged by God and Yelp alike

Origin Story:

The disorder began around age 12, when she was forced to choose between chicken nuggets and mac & cheese at a Chili's.
Her parents divorced shortly afterward.
She still blames the nuggets.

Over time, the symptoms evolved:

- Panic when the menu has too many fonts
- Rage when "gluten-free" has an upcharge
- Whispering *"What are you getting?"* to the entire table like it's a sacred ritual

She once stood in front of a taco truck menu so long the owner asked if she was waiting for a sign from the universe.
She said:

"I'm hoping for one."

Case Study: Lunch with Friends

At a recent girls' brunch, Brittany reviewed the menu for 11 minutes and then asked the server:

Jamison Carrier

"What's your vibe on the French toast?"

When asked to clarify, she said:

"Like… is it emotional French toast or just, like, regular?"

She then ordered pancakes. Changed her mind mid-sentence.
Then whispered, *"No, wait…"* as the server walked away.

When the food arrived, she stared at her plate, looked at her friend's, and softly said:

"I should've gotten what you got."

Her friend had a bowl of plain oatmeal.

Therapist's Interpretation:

This is not about food.
This is about identity.

Each menu item is a portal into a parallel life.
Brittany doesn't know who she is—so she doesn't know what to eat.

- Salad? She's clean, disciplined, likable.
- Burger? She's carefree, fun, too much.
- Avocado toast? She's basic.
- Avocado toast with hot honey and pickled radish? She's trying too hard.

It's not lunch.
It's a personality crisis on a plate.

Treatment Plan:

1. **Pre-Menu Meditation**
   One deep breath per appetizer option.
2. **Hard Menu Caps**
   Choose in under 3 minutes or let the server decide.
3. **Menu Item Identity Desensitization**
   Weekly exercises where Brittany orders something she normally wouldn't.
   Her first trial? Turkey club sandwich.
   She cried. But she ate it. And survived.
4. **Therapy Phrase of the Week**

   "It's just lunch. I am not my sandwich."

Self-Assessment: MDP

"I should've gotten what you got."

1. When handed a menu, your first move is to:
A. Scan it and order what looks good
B. Ask questions about ingredients
C. Whisper "What are you getting?" to the group
D. Freeze like a hostage and say "You go first"

2. You place your order and immediately feel:
A. Confident
B. Neutral
C. Mild regret
D. Crippling doubt and food envy

3. When the food arrives, you:
A. Dig in and enjoy it

B. Check your order against the photo online
C. Stare longingly at someone else's plate
D. Say "I knew I should've gotten that" with actual sorrow

4. Your most used restaurant phrase is:
A. "Looks good!"
B. "Can I sub that?"
C. "Ugh, I should've picked what you picked."
D. "Let's just split everything. I can't commit."

Mostly C's or D's?
You've got Menu Decision Paralysis.
It's not about the meal—it's about existential doubt.
But hey, at least you didn't order the side salad with no dressing. Probably.

Doctor's Notes:

Brittany is making slow progress.
She now reviews menus before arriving.
Last week, she ordered nachos on the first try.
Her boyfriend wept with pride.

We'll be monitoring for future episodes, especially with new cuisine genres and the dreaded *build-your-own-bowl* situation.

Next week, she'll face her biggest test yet: ordering from a food truck with a chalkboard menu and no pictures.

We are hopeful.
And lightly terrified.

Syndromedy

Chapter Five

Emotional Soft Launching Syndrome (ESLS)

"All feelings must be disguised as memes, song lyrics, or 'haha kinda true.'"

Patient: Kayla M.
Age: 21
Occupation: Content Creator / Subtext Strategist
Referral Source: Her roommate, who finally snapped and said, "Just say what you mean, or hand me a decoder ring."

Session Notes:

Kayla arrived wearing sunglasses indoors.
Not for fashion—she'd been "crying but not like crying-crying."

She showed me her latest Instagram story:
A screenshot of lyrics from a Taylor Swift song with no caption.

"It's not about anyone," she said.
Then added, "But if they see it, they'll know."

Classic ESLS.

When asked how she was doing, she said:

"I mean, I've posted some things. You'll get the vibe."

Symptoms Include:

- Communicating emotional states exclusively through:
    - Curated playlists
    - Poetic TikToks
    - Moody Pinterest boards
    - Song lyrics from 2009
- Frequently saying, "It's not about them," while furiously watching their views on her story
- Leaving cryptic captions like:
    - "Energy doesn't lie."
    - "Protect your peace."
    - "Grateful for the ones who stayed." *(Three people tagged. No explanation.)*

When asked directly how she felt, Kayla replied:

"It's in the reel, if you watched it all the way through."

Notable Behavior:

After a painful breakup, Kayla did not tell her friends directly.
Instead, she posted the following over 24 hours:

- An Instagram story of a burning rose
- A meme that said "Closure is a scam"
- A black square with the caption:

> "Letting go doesn't mean you're
> weak. It means you're woke."

- A 19-second acoustic cover of
  "Unanswered Prayers"

A concerned friend texted:

"Are you okay?"
She replied:
"Haha totally, just vibing 🤍"

Then posted another reel the next morning titled:
"Growth."

Therapist's Interpretation:

Emotional Soft Launching Syndrome is a modern
defense mechanism.
It's not avoidance—it's *performance.*
A way to express hurt, anger, or longing while
remaining publicly ambiguous and emotionally
unaccountable.

The ESLS patient doesn't want to talk about it.
They want you to *notice* they're not talking about
it.
Then reach out.
Then decode it.
Then maybe never bring it up again.

Treatment Plan:

1. **Full Sentence Honesty Practice**
   Say what you're feeling... *in your own words.*
   (Kayla broke into hives.)

2. **Story Cleanse**
   No cryptic posts for seven days.
   No song lyrics unless it's karaoke.
3. **Direct Communication Drills**
   Text someone what you feel *without* a
   meme attached.
4. **Caption Restraint Training**
   No more than one emotionally charged
   quote per month.
   Quotes from Pinterest are considered a
   relapse.
5. **Therapy Phrase of the Week**

   "I can be honest, even if it's
   awkward."

Self-Assessment: ESLS

"It's not a subtweet if you pretend it's not."

1. When upset, you're most likely to:
A. Text a close friend directly
B. Journal or go for a walk
C. Post a meme that says "People change. Moon
phases don't."
D. Share lyrics from a sad girl playlist, then turn
off read receipts

**2. Someone texts: "Are you okay?" You
respond with:**
A. "Honestly, not really."
B. "Getting there."
C. "Totally fine lol 🩶 "
D. "Haha just tired. New post up tho 👀 "

3. You've posted something that made a specific person text:
A. "Are you okay?"
B. "Was that about me?"
C. "Yikes."
D. *Nothing—but they viewed it 12 times and you screenshotted it.*

4. You describe your current mood as:
A. Clear and honest
B. Bit off but manageable
C. "Main character energy, kinda broken"
D. *A blurry selfie with the caption: "Healing."*

Mostly C's or D's?
You're not just feeling things. You're *covertly communicating* your pain.
You've got ESLS.
Say it out loud—we'll wait. No meme required.

Doctor's Notes:

Kayla made progress this week.
She sent an actual text to a friend saying, "I'm having a rough day."

No emojis.
No Spotify link.
Just feelings.

She cried. Her friend called.
They talked.

She didn't post about it.
That's growth.

PART II: Domestic Dysfunction

Because You Definitely Married Someone with Opposite Settings

Chapter Six

Situational Object Blindness Disorder (SOBD)

"Where's the Ranch?" It's in front of your face, Chad.

Patient: Chad R.
Age: 41
Occupation: Amateur Fridge Yeller / Drawer Opener / Husband
Referral Source: His wife, who found the Ranch dressing in under four seconds

Session Notes:

Chad arrived five minutes late and said he "couldn't find the building."
It was labeled. With a sign. And a balloon.

When I asked if he'd looked carefully, he said,

"I did! I swear it wasn't there before."

His intake form was incomplete.
Why?

"I didn't see that last page."

Classic SOBD.

Symptoms Include:

Jamison Carrier

- Staring into a full fridge while asking where something is
- Opening one cabinet and immediately giving up
- Uttering the phrase:

> "It's not in there. I checked."
> (He did not check.)

- Weaponizing helplessness in domestic spaces
- Expecting location-based miracles from a spouse, roommate, or mother

In a recent episode, Chad spent five minutes searching for a remote that was:

- On the armrest
- Touching his leg
- Glowing

Notable Incident:

Chad once texted his wife from the kitchen:

"Where's the mustard?"

She replied:

"Fridge door. Second shelf."

He sent a photo of the fridge.
She circled the mustard in red.
He responded:

"Weird. I didn't see it."

She was upstairs.
She still saw it.

Therapist's Interpretation:

Situational Object Blindness Disorder is a neurological reflex triggered by minor inconvenience.
The brain momentarily shuts down visual processing when the stakes are low and help is nearby.

Translation:
Chad doesn't look harder because he knows someone else will.

This is not about poor vision.
It's about low-stakes surrender.

Left untreated, SOBD can evolve into advanced phases:

- Lost keys on forehead
- Glasses in hand
- Asking for towels while standing next to the towel rack

Treatment Plan:

1. **Five-Second Pause Protocol**
   Patient must stare at the area for a full five seconds before yelling for help.
   (Chad hates this.)
2. **Point & Scan Practice**
   Practice looking *with intent*, not just

45

opening and glancing like a confused prairie dog.

3. **Verbal Accountability Reframe**
   Replace "It's not there" with "I don't see it yet."
4. **Blindfold Therapy**
   Chad was blindfolded and still found the mustard faster when he actually tried.
5. **Therapy Phrase of the Week**

"If I open it, I will actually look."

Self-Assessment: SOBD

"It's not here." – You, while standing in front of it.

1. When looking for something, you usually:
A. Scan the area thoroughly
B. Move a few things around
C. Glance vaguely and give up
D. Shout the name of the item like it might respond

2. When someone finds what you couldn't, you say:
A. "Ah, there it is."
B. "How did I miss that?"
C. "It wasn't there a second ago."
D. "You must've moved it."

3. Your most used phrase during any search is:
A. "Let me look again."
B. "Hold on."
C. "I can't find it."

D. "It's gone. It doesn't exist. We've been robbed."

4. You're most likely to miss an object that is:
A. Buried or hidden
B. Behind something
C. In plain sight
D. Literally in your hand

Mostly C's or D's?
You may have Situational Object Blindness Disorder.
You're not broken. You're just looking with vibes, not vision.
The Ranch was always there. We promise.

Doctor's Notes:

Chad has started taking a full 10 seconds before asking his wife where something is.
He found the ketchup last week with no assistance.

It was exactly where she said it would be.

She cried.
Chad took a victory lap.

We are cautiously optimistic.

Chapter Seven

Default No Disorder (DND)

"If joy is suggested, your instinct is to block it."

Patient: Kyle B.
Age: 35
Occupation: Human Break Pedal / Fun Sponge
(recovering)
Referral Source: His friend group, who started
planning things without him

Session Notes:

Kyle's opening statement:

"I just don't like committing to things I might
regret enjoying."

When invited to dinner, the first response is
always:

"Ugh. I don't know. That feels like… a lot."

We explored what "a lot" means.
Turns out it was:

- A 6:00 p.m. reservation
- 3 friends
- Within 4 miles of home

Kyle is not allergic to joy.
He just needs **three weeks' notice** and **zero
enthusiasm.**

Symptoms Include:

- Reflexively saying "no" to any social invitation
- Needing a full 24-hour notice to consider brunch
- Getting annoyed when people seem too excited
- Asking, "Who all's going?" as a threat
- Describing fun things as "draining" without attending

Kyle once declined a friend's birthday party because it was on a *Thursday.*
He does not work Fridays.
He just didn't feel "emotionally organized" for it.

Notable Incident:

A friend once invited Kyle to a spontaneous game night.

He responded with:

"Game night?? On a *weeknight*?? You're unwell."

The friend said,

"It's just Uno and pizza."

Kyle replied:

"I can't mentally prepare for Uno right now."

Therapist's Interpretation:

Jamison Carrier

Default No Disorder is a behavioral protection response.
It is not about the event.
It's about risk: emotional, social, and energy-based.

The DND patient fears:

- Overstimulation
- Underdressing
- Laughing too hard at something he secretly enjoys
- Being asked to play Pictionary with strangers

The "No" is a buffer.
It gives him time to negotiate with his own resistance.

Ironically, once there?
He has a great time.
He just won't admit it until Tuesday.

Treatment Plan:

1. **Yes-by-Default Rewiring**
   Say "Yes" first. Regret it later.
   (Revolutionary.)
2. **Surprise Exposure Therapy**
   Attend one spontaneous event per month without full control of logistics.
3. **Affirmation Practice**
   Repeat: "Joy is not a trap."
4. **Pause + Reframe**
   When invited, pause 5 seconds before

responding.
(Kyle once twitched.)

5. **Therapy Phrase of the Week**

"Fun is allowed. Even on weekdays."

Self-Assessment: DND

"I'll let you know… maybe… I'm leaning toward no."

1. You're invited to an impromptu dinner. Your reaction is:
A. "Sounds fun!"
B. "Let me check."
C. "Ugh, I'm already tired tomorrow."
D. "Why would you do this to me?"

2. Someone texts "Game night tonight?" You respond:
A. "I'm in!"
B. "Who's going?"
C. "Absolutely not."
D. *No response. You open the blinds slightly to make sure they didn't show up.*

3. You've described karaoke night as:
A. A blast
B. A lot
C. A trap
D. Emotional terrorism

4. Your most-used calendar phrase is:
A. "Blocked for fun!"
B. "Flexible"
C. "Please no"

Jamison Carrier

D. *All-day event titled: "Stay Home & Reboot My Personality"*

Mostly C's or D's?

You've got Default No Disorder.
You're not anti-social. You're just emotionally high-maintenance.
We get it. But we're still picking you up at 6:00.

Doctor's Notes:

Kyle attended a birthday party last week.
He stayed for over an hour.
He even smiled.

He claimed it was "fine."
The photos say otherwise.

We're calling it progress.
He's calling it a fluke.

Either way... he's on the list for next time.

Chapter Eight

Checklist Addiction Syndrome (CAS)

"You wrote it down just to check it off. Again."

Patient: Melissa T.
Age: 38
Occupation: Professional Organizer / Checkbox Enthusiast
Referral Source: Her husband, who found "Shower" on her to-do list—with a checkmark

Session Notes:

Melissa arrived early.
She pulled a leather-bound planner from her tote, opened it with reverence, and said:

"So… should I log this as 'Therapy' or 'Emotional Maintenance'?"

She then crossed it off.
The session had not yet begun.

She is not unwell.
She is simply *thriving… in list format.*

Symptoms Include:

- Writes down tasks she's already completed just to check them off
- Treats planner like a sacred scroll

- Has three calendars: paper, digital, and dry-erase
- Uses checkboxes to regulate dopamine
- Describes an unfinished list as "emotionally itchy"

Melissa once rewrote an entire day's list because the original layout didn't spark joy.
She refers to pens by their brand names.
She has a favorite highlighter color for "mild urgency."

Notable Incident:

After a day of unplanned interruptions, Melissa was visibly agitated.

I asked what was wrong.
She opened her planner and said:

"I didn't get to check off *'breathe.'*"

I said,

"But… you're breathing."

She replied,

"Not according to the list."

Therapist's Interpretation:

Checklist Addiction Syndrome is a highly functional hangup.

Jamison Carrier

It provides structure, clarity, and a manufactured sense of control in a chaotic world.

For the CAS patient, the checkbox is not just a tool—it's a reward system.
A serotonin faucet.
A paper-based form of inner peace.

Left unchecked (pun intended), CAS can lead to:

- Over-scheduling
- Calendar worship
- Passive-aggressiveness toward spontaneous people
- Resentment toward "free-spirited" humans who simply exist without OneNote

Treatment Plan:

1. **Unscheduled Hour Trial**
   Block out one hour per week labeled only:
   "???"
   (Melissa dry-heaved.)
2. **Completed-Task Restraint**
   Do not add completed tasks to the list just to check them off.
   (She wrote this down. Then crossed it off.)
3. **Checkbox Moderation**
   Limit to 20 boxes per day. No "sub-lists of sub-lists."
4. **Spontaneity Rewiring**
   Leave one task open-ended.
   Example: "Fun (TBD)"
5. **Therapy Phrase of the Week**

"I am not my productivity. I am not my pen."

Self-Assessment: CAS

"Just crossing this off real quick…"

1. When you complete a task that wasn't on your list, you:
A. Move on
B. Mentally note it
C. Add it to the list just to check it off
D. Add it, check it off, highlight it, and announce it to the room

2. You describe your planner as:
A. Helpful
B. Optional
C. Sacred
D. My second brain (please don't touch it)

3. Someone cancels plans last minute. You respond by:
A. Flexing and rescheduling
B. Slight disappointment
C. Deep resentment
D. Writing "Cancelled" in neat handwriting and pretending you're fine

4. Your most-used productivity app feature is:
A. Calendar sync
B. Reminders
C. Daily checklists
D. All of the above + color-coded categories + backup bullet journal

Jamison Carrier

Mostly C's or D's?
You've got Checklist Addiction Syndrome.
You're not broken. You're just a walking
spreadsheet with feelings.
And yes—reading this chapter counts.

Doctor's Notes:

Melissa now practices leaving one checkbox
unmarked each week.
It causes mild internal screaming.
But she hasn't died yet.

Next step: spontaneous lunch.

We will write it down.
And yes… she can check it off afterward.

Chapter Nine

Compulsive Vacation Itinerary Syndrome (CVIS)

"We can rest when we die."

Patient: Jamison C.
Age: Lifetime diagnosis
Occupation: Vacation Strategist / Efficiency Evangelist
Referral Source: His wife, who just wanted to sit by the pool without a laminated schedule

Session Notes:

Jamison grew up believing that vacation was not rest. It was a mission. A test of planning precision. A race to see *everything an area had to offer,* preferably by lunch.

He arrived at his first joint vacation with his wife, Kathy, armed with:

- A color-coded itinerary
- Printed attraction hours
- Backup options for inclement weather
- Bathroom break windows

His excitement was palpable.
Her face said: *"What is happening?"*

Kathy, raised on the concept of **vacations as rest**, was not prepared to be briefed at 6:45 a.m.

on a day that ended with the phrase *"sunset kayak experience (optional but encouraged)."*

She just wanted to *sit*.

Jamison paced beside the lounge chair.

Symptoms Include:

- Referring to hotel breakfast as "fueling time"
- Scheduling scenic overlooks with 10-minute max viewing windows
- Using phrases like:
    - "We didn't *do* anything today."
    - "Daylight's a burnin'."
    - "This line is eating into our lunch block."
- Carrying a backpack with printed confirmations, backup ponchos, and a portable phone charger labeled *Plan B*

Origin Story:

The disorder began in childhood, during family trips packed tighter than a TSA-approved carry-on.
Each trip was an event.
Each day: accounted for.

Time was to be **maximized.**
Regret was to be **eliminated.**

By age 13, Jamison could recite the entire Dollywood show schedule from memory.

Jamison Carrier

By 16, he was managing multi-family lake house weekends with the precision of a military contractor.

He believed *free time* was just poorly allocated opportunity.

Case Study: The First Vacation with Kathy

Jamison had mapped out a week of sights, hikes, and dinner reservations with the efficiency of a travel concierge having a midlife breakthrough.

The itinerary was a color-coded Excel spreadsheet titled:
"Vacation Master Plan – Final FINAL (v7)."
It included estimated drive times, weather projections, and a note in cell F14 that read:
"Quick scenic overlook – 9 min max."

He printed two copies and laminated one—just in case.

Kathy brought sunscreen.

On day two, while Jamison was briefing her on zipline timing and "optional" cave tours, she interrupted with a sentence no scheduler is prepared to hear:

"I don't want to *do* anything today."

Jamison blinked twice.
Checked the itinerary.
Then said:

"I scheduled an afternoon nap at 2:45."

Therapist's Interpretation:

CVIS is not about travel.
It's about control.

The compulsive scheduler believes relaxation can
only be *earned* through rigorous activity.
Downtime is waste.
Spontaneity is risk.
Unstructured time feels like failure.

Ironically, they don't even enjoy most of the
scheduled events.
They enjoy *having scheduled them.*

It's not a vacation.
It's a productivity pilgrimage.

Treatment Plan:

1. **Mandatory Lounge Time**
    Sit for one full hour without a plan. No
    researching Yelp. No pacing.
2. **Unscheduled Day Test**
    Leave one vacation day fully unplanned.
    (Kathy called this "Tuesday.")
3. **Schedule Desensitization**
    Practice hearing the phrase "I don't want
    to do anything today" without clenching
    your jaw.
4. **Perspective Rewiring**
    View your spouse's nap not as betrayal,
    but as restoration.

5. **Therapy Phrase of the Week**

"Presence is not a missed
opportunity. It is the point."

Self-Assessment: CVIS

"Just a few quick stops. Should only take six hours."

1. When planning a trip, you:
A. Book a flight and figure it out later
B. Have a few ideas, but stay flexible
C. Create a shared Google calendar
D. Build a daily itinerary titled "Master Plan v3
FINAL FINAL (revised)"

2. You describe a successful vacation as:
A. Restful
B. Enjoyable
C. Productive
D. Completed with a laminated checklist

3. Your spouse or travel companion has said:
A. "That was fun."
B. "That was relaxing."
C. "That was… a lot."
D. "I feel like I just got off a game show."

4. Your most-used phrase while traveling is:
A. "Let's see where the day takes us."
B. "Let's keep it loose."
C. "Let's stay on track."
D. "If we leave now, we can make the 1:15 tour
AND still see the overlook before dinner."

Mostly C's or D's?
You may have CVIS.
Your family still loves you.
They just don't want to hike at dawn. Again.

Doctor's Notes:

Jamison is learning to schedule *less*.
His new itinerary template includes one
revolutionary category: *"Do nothing."*

He and Kathy are still married.
But on their next trip, she booked the Airbnb.
And told him the Wi-Fi was down.

He didn't check.

That's progress.

Chapter Ten

Amazon Box Blindness (ABB)

"You bought it. You forgot it. It's in the laundry room."

Patient: Val M.
Age: 45
Occupation: Passive Package Collector / Label Ignorer
Referral Source: Her husband, Tim, who tripped over a third box of "emergency flashlights"

Session Notes:

Val arrived 10 minutes late.
She blamed traffic.
Her phone later revealed she was home…
opening a box she "didn't remember ordering."

When asked what was inside, she said,

"Honestly? No idea. I think batteries. Or kitchen scissors. Maybe a dog puzzle."

Classic ABB.

Symptoms Include:

- Receiving multiple Amazon packages per week and claiming they're "household essentials"
- Leaving unopened boxes in:
  - The laundry room
  - The garage

- o A chair, now no one can sit in
- Describing delivery day as "Christmas, but with more guilt"
- Using vague phrases like:
  - o "It was on sale."
  - o "I meant to return that."
  - o "It's a backup."
  - o "It's for camping."

Val once found a second electric toothbrush she didn't remember ordering.
She kept both.
"You never know," she said.
She is not a dentist.

Notable Incident:

After a garage cleanout, Val discovered:

- Four boxes of air filters
- Two wireless doorbells
- A churro maker
- A water bottle with her name on it
  She has never made churros.
  She drinks bottled water from a plastic bottle.

When asked about the duplicates, she said:

"I think Amazon glitched."
Spoiler: It did not.

Therapist's Interpretation:

Jamison Carrier

Amazon Box Blindness is a modern disorder rooted in convenience, consumer amnesia, and stress-based consumer click therapy.

For ABB patients, the act of ordering provides a dopamine hit.
The delivery? A tiny high.
The follow-through? Completely unnecessary.

It's not about the item.
It's about control… disguised as utility… buried in cardboard.

Treatment Plan:

1. **The "One In, One Out" Rule**
   Nothing new enters the home until an old item is removed.
   (Val cried.)
2. **Delayed Purchase Protocol**
   Wait 24 hours before buying non-essential items.
   Bonus: The thing will be in the cart, silently judging you.
3. **The Box Opening Ceremony**
   Each box must be opened, acknowledged, and assigned a purpose within 24 hours.
4. **Return Window Accountability Partner**
   A designated person to remind Val the return window closes in 8 days.
5. **Therapy Phrase of the Week**

   "It's not a deal if I forget I bought it."

Self-Assessment: ABB

"What's in that box?" – You, to yourself, in your own home.

1. You've opened a package and said:
A. "Perfect, it's here."
B. "I forgot about this!"
C. "What… is this?"
D. "Huh. Did I order this? Did someone send this?"

2. You currently have unopened boxes in your home. You feel:
A. Organized
B. Indifferent
C. Slightly ashamed
D. Like you might be on a documentary

3. You justify new purchases by saying:
A. "We need it."
B. "It's cheaper than in stores."
C. "I might use it someday."
D. "Look how much I saved."

4. You once re-bought something because:
A. Yours broke
B. You wanted a backup
C. You forgot you already had it
D. You couldn't find it under the other boxes

Mostly C's or D's?
You've got ABB.
You don't have a storage issue.
You have an awareness issue.
And a churro maker.

Jamison Carrier

Doctor's Notes:

Val opened four boxes this week.
Two were duplicate items.
One was a sleep mask with Bluetooth.
One was a dog vest.

She has no dog.

But she *did* return the dog vest.

Progress.

Syndromedy

Jamison Carrier

PART III: Fitness Delusion & Performance Theater

Where Self-Improvement Meets Vanity in Moisture-Wicking Fabric

Chapter Eleven

Sweatless Gym Attendance Syndrome (SGAS)

"You go every day. Your body has no idea."

Patient: Trent D.
Age: 32
Occupation: Fitness Presence Specialist / Mirror Wiper / Gym Regular (emotionally)
Referral Source: His roommate, who noted, "He's been 'working out' for three years and still gets winded walking up our stairs."

Session Notes:

Trent entered the session in gym clothes so clean they squeaked, clutching a protein shake like a security blanket.

When asked how his workouts were going, he said:

"Great. I'm in the gym six days a week."

When asked what he *does* there, he replied:

"You know… mobility… core… vibe checks."

When pressed further, he admitted to:

- 12–15 minutes of stretching

73

Jamison Carrier

- One machine (low resistance)
- Three mirror selfies
- Socializing
- A recovery smoothie

He hasn't broke a sweat since July.
Of 2021.

Symptoms Include:

- Wearing gym clothes more often than regular clothes
- Treating the gym as a second office or therapy center
- Documenting workouts without actual exertion
- Phrases include:
    - "I'm working on my form."
    - "I'm building a base."
    - "I'm going light today… and most days."

Trent once skipped a leg workout because he said the gym had 'hostile energy'

Notable Incident:

Trent once posted a workout video titled "Push Day Grind 💪"
The video showed:

- A half-hearted shoulder shrug
- A sip of water
- 43 seconds of flexing to check lighting

The post got 78 likes.
He captioned it:

"Putting in the work when no one's watching."
Everyone watched.
No one was inspired.

Therapist's Interpretation:

Sweatless Gym Attendance Syndrome is a performance-based identity disorder rooted in the *idea* of fitness rather than the experience of it.

The SGAS patient isn't chasing gains.
He's chasing **aesthetic accountability.**

He believes:

- Gym attendance = moral superiority
- Owning pre-workout justifies skipping cardio
- Wearing a lifting belt to do curls builds credibility

This is fitness theater.
Effort is optional.
Presence is everything.

Treatment Plan:

1. **Actual Sweat Requirement**
   Must break a visible sweat within first 20 minutes.
   (Trent brought cologne.)

2. **Selfie Moratorium**
   No gym selfies for 30 days.
   He may still post smoothies—but must
   disclose their contents.
3. **Cardio Reintroduction Protocol**
   Begin with light jog. Graduate to "feeling
   your lungs."
4. **Accountability Buddy (Real, Not
   Digital)**
   Partner must confirm workout occurred
   and involved effort.
5. **Therapy Phrase of the Week**

   "If my watch didn't log it, and my
   shirt isn't wet—I probably didn't
   work out."

Self-Assessment: SGAS

"I train hard… on Instagram."

1. Your gym bag contains:
A. Shoes, towel, and water
B. Protein bars and resistance bands
C. Tripod and ring light
D. More outfits than reps

2. After a workout, you usually feel:
A. Exhausted
B. Strong
C. Lightly dewy
D. Ready for a content drop

3. Your favorite part of the gym is:
A. The treadmill
B. The weight bench

C. The mirrors
D. The parking lot (for post-gym selfies)

4. You believe fitness is:
A. A journey of health
B. A way to challenge yourself
C. A brand
D. Something you can imply without actually doing

Mostly C's or D's?
You may have SGAS.
You don't need new shoes.
You need to sweat.
And maybe—just maybe—lift something heavier than your phone.

Doctor's Notes:

Trent is starting slow.
He jogged one lap last week and mistook a real sweat for an allergic reaction.

He now knows:
Effort isn't the enemy.
Authenticity weighs more than dumbbells.

We're calling it... active progress.

Chapter Twelve

Workout Identity Projection Disorder (WIPD)

"I ran 7 miles this morning." — You, to the mailman.

Patient: Jason R.
Age: 41
Occupation: Personal Branding Hobbyist / Lifestyle Bragger
Referral Source: His coworker, who asked how his weekend was and got a full breakdown of his heart rate zones

Session Notes:

Jason didn't sit down right away.
He stood tall, slightly flexing, and said:

"Sorry, I'm a little stiff—I hit legs this morning."

He then placed his gallon water jug on the table like it needed to hydrate, too.

He was not asked.
No one mentioned fitness.
It's just who he is.

Symptoms Include:

- Announces workouts unprompted in conversations, texts, and voicemail greetings

- Refers to food as "fuel"
- Describes soreness as a badge of honor
- Will find a way to mention:
  - Mileage
  - Lifting stats
  - Resting heart rate
  - That one time he did a Tough Mudder

Jason once mentioned his macros during a funeral luncheon.
It was not about him.
Until it was.

Notable Incident:

Jason was at a 4th of July BBQ when someone asked how work was going.
He responded with:

"Great, thanks. Ran five miles this morning, then hit chest and tris."

No follow-up question was asked.
He added:

"I track everything in Garmin now. Apple Watch just wasn't getting my V02 max right."

Someone offered him a burger.
He declined.
But talked for 11 minutes about *why*.

Jamison Carrier
Therapist's Interpretation:

Workout Identity Projection Disorder is rooted in
the need to be seen as disciplined, superior, and in
control—even if that control comes at the cost of
every social interaction.

The WIPD patient's body is no longer just a
body.
It's a brand.

He doesn't train for wellness.
He trains for acknowledgment.

He sees rest days as weakness.
He sees silence as a missed opportunity to say "I
do CrossFit."

Treatment Plan:

1. **Conversation Cleanse**
   Go one full day without referencing your
   workout.
   If symptoms persist, extend to 48 hours.
2. **Social Humility Drills**
   Practice saying, "I'm good," without
   adding, "just a little sore from push day."
3. **Burger Desensitization Therapy**
   Attend a cookout. Eat a normal burger.
   Do not mention macros.
4. **Mental Reps**
   For every time you want to mention a
   workout, say something encouraging to
   someone else.
5. **Therapy Phrase of the Week**

"My value is not measured in
steps, sweat, or protein powder."

Self-Assessment: WIPD

"It's not about attention. But if you ask…"

1. You're introduced to someone new. You say:
A. "Nice to meet you."
B. "What do you do?"
C. "I run a little."
D. "I just got back from leg day. Sorry if I'm limping."

2. Your social media feed includes:
A. Friends and family
B. News and hobbies
C. Protein brands and running maps
D. Screenshots of your fitness tracker with a caption like "Just getting started 💪"

3. You once texted a friend:
A. "Let's catch up!"
B. "You good?"
C. "Just crushed back and bis. Feeling alive."
D. A mirror selfie captioned "no filter, just focus"

4. Your spouse has said:
A. "I'm proud of you."
B. "You're so consistent."
C. "Do you ever stop talking about working out?"
D. "This is why we can't have dinner with normal people."

Jamison Carrier

Mostly C's or D's?
You've got WIPD.
Your discipline is impressive.
Your grip on social awareness? Slightly less
defined.

Doctor's Notes:

Jason is trying.
He made it 19 hours without referencing his
workout.

He then complimented someone's dog and
followed it with, "He's got great form. I say that
as someone who deadlifts."

Still… we're calling it progress.
And no one cried during burger therapy.
Which, for WIPD, is basically a miracle.

Syndromedy

Chapter Thirteen

Aspirational Accessory Syndrome (AAS)

"Looking good is more important than being good."

Patient: Heather N.
Age: 36
Occupation: Hobby Enthusiast / Pre-Workout Shopper
Referral Source: Her credit card company, which flagged seven Backcountry purchases in two days

Session Notes:

Heather arrived in full pickleball attire.
She does not play pickleball.
She "looked into it" last week after hearing someone at church mention it.

She now owns:

- Two custom paddles
- Matching moisture-wicking sets
- A visor
- Court shoes
- An insulated water bottle with a built-in speaker

When asked if she's played yet, she said:

"No, but I'm emotionally ready."

Symptoms Include:

- Buys top-tier gear before attempting the activity
- Has strong opinions about apparel "must-haves" for things she's never done
- Will say things like:
    o "You can't skimp on quality."
    o "I'm investing in the experience."
    o "You have to dress the part."
- Believes looking capable *will* lead to being capable

Heather once bought an entire camping setup—including a rooftop tent, enamel cookware, and a branded headlamp—then booked a cabin.

She called it:

"Glamping with integrity."

Notable Incident:

Heather expressed interest in cycling.
Within a week, she owned:

- A carbon fiber bike
- Clip-in shoes
- Padded shorts
- A helmet with integrated Bluetooth
- Matching gloves
- An app subscription
- A repair kit (unused)

When asked how far she'd ridden, she replied:

Jamison Carrier

"Technically zero. But I *felt* like a cyclist all week."

Therapist's Interpretation:

Aspirational Accessory Syndrome is driven by performance anxiety mixed with aesthetic commitment.

The AAS patient hopes gear will compensate for:

- Lack of experience
- Fear of failure
- Needing to look like they know what they're doing

It's retail confidence therapy.
Their closet is a museum of half-started ambitions.

It's not about doing the thing.
It's about **looking like the kind of person who does the thing.**

Treatment Plan:

1. **Trial Period Protocol**
   No purchases until you've committed to the activity for at least two weeks
2. **Rent Before You Flex**
   Use loaner gear. Prove interest before swiping.
3. **Postpone the Look**
   You're not less committed if your outfit isn't coordinated

4. **The "Are You Good at This Yet?" Test**
Ask: "Have I practiced this more than I've shopped for it?"

5. **Therapy Phrase of the Week**

> "The paddle doesn't make the player. The player makes the purchase *after* learning to play."

Self-Assessment: AAS

"I'm not doing it yet, but I have the jacket."

1. You've bought gear for an activity you haven't done. You justify it by saying:
A. "I'll grow into it."
B. "This motivates me."
C. "You've got to have the right setup."
D. "It was 30% off. I'm basically saving money."

2. You currently own equipment for:
A. One active hobby
B. Two or three occasional interests
C. At least five sports or lifestyle trends
D. An entire Bass Pro Shops aisle

3. You see someone posting about hiking. You think:
A. "That's nice."
B. "Maybe I'll try that."
C. "I should get hiking boots."
D. *Already in checkout with trekking poles and a hydration vest*

4. Your significant other has said:
A. "You're so adventurous."

B. "You try new things."
C. "Do you actually *use* any of this?"
D. "We need a second garage."

Mostly C's or D's?
You may have AAS.
You're not a fraud.
You're just dressing for the life you haven't
started living yet.

Doctor's Notes:

Heather has agreed to wait 30 days before buying
stand-up paddleboard gear.
She did, however, buy a swimsuit "just in case."
And a waterproof phone pouch.
And a visor.

We're calling that… halfway there.

Syndromedy

Chapter Fourteen

Checklist-Based Fitness Validation (CFV)

"If it's not on Strava, did it even happen?"

Patient: Morgan K.
Age: 29
Occupation: Digital Accountability Addict /
Metrics Missionary
Referral Source: Her smartwatch, which
triggered a wellness notification that read:
"You've walked 12,000 steps but made zero eye
contact today."

Session Notes:

Morgan tracks everything.

Steps.
Heart rate.
Sleep score.
Recovery status.
Calories burned by thinking about exercising.

When asked how she *feels,* she checks her phone
and says:

"Honestly? My readiness score is a 92 today."

She logs walks, yoga, and hydration.
She's considered manually entering the effort it
takes to argue with her insurance company.

If her watch dies mid-run, she'll start over.
If the gym Wi-Fi is down, she leaves.

Symptoms Include:

- Will not count a workout unless it's tracked
- Shares stats publicly and says "just keeping myself accountable"
- Feels a deep emotional attachment to the "streak"
- Has said:
  - "I can't lose my progress."
  - "If I skip today, the graph dips."
  - "It's not obsession. It's consistency."

Morgan once walked around her apartment at 11:57 p.m. to hit her daily step goal.
In socks.

Notable Incident:

Morgan forgot to hit "Start" on her fitness app before a 6-mile run.

After a full panic spiral, she posted:

"Ran 6 miles but forgot to track it so I guess it didn't happen 😫 "

She then ran 2 more.
Just to log it.

She captioned the second run:

Jamison Carrier

"Mental toughness is real."

Therapist's Interpretation:

Checklist-Based Fitness Validation is not about health.
It's about **proof.**

CFV patients don't move for movement's sake.
They move for metrics, graphs, and streaks.
Validation is not internal—it's cloud-based.

Their real workout is *achieving closure* by checking a digital box.

Treatment Plan:

1. **Unplugged Workout Trial**
   Complete one workout with no tracking device.
   (Morgan needed a support person.)
2. **Streak Surrender**
   Miss one day intentionally.
   Write down your feelings. Don't post them.
3. **Non-Digital Wins**
   Journal how you felt after the workout instead of what your watch said
4. **Mute the Metrics**
   Turn off "You didn't close your rings!" notifications.
   You are not a hamster.
5. **Therapy Phrase of the Week**

   "Progress is real—even if your watch didn't see it."

Self-Assessment: CFV

"I'm not addicted. I'm accountable."

1. You missed your daily goal by 1%. You:
A. Shrug it off
B. Try again tomorrow
C. Feel mild shame
D. Pace around the house while brushing your teeth

2. When someone asks how your workout was, you:
A. Say how you felt
B. Say what you did
C. Say your stats
D. Show them your phone while flexing slightly

3. You've said "I can't stop now" because:
A. You were improving
B. You were in the zone
C. The app said so
D. You had a streak to protect

4. If you forget to log a workout, you:
A. Don't care
B. Are a little annoyed
C. Try to approximate it later
D. Wonder if you even exist

Mostly C's or D's?
You may have CFV.
You're not training your body.
You're training your tracker.

And it's time to take your identity off the cloud.

Jamison Carrier

Doctor's Notes:

Morgan went for a walk without her watch.
She kept checking her wrist like a confused
alpaca.
But she did it.

Next up: yoga.
No playlist.
No stats.
Just… existing.

We're terrified. But hopeful.

Chapter Fifteen

Mental Fortitude Denial Syndrome (MFDS)

"You're not sick. You have a weak mind."

Patient: Derek J.
Age: 47
Occupation: Amateur Tough Guy / Weakness Denier / Cold Plunge Evangelist
Referral Source: His 12-year-old son, after Derek told him to "walk it off" when he broke his ankle

Session Notes:

Derek walked in with a slight limp.
He claimed it was "from leg day."
It was actually a bone bruise from trying to prove he could still dunk.

He waved off any concern with:

"Pain is just the body whining."
Then added:
"That's not scientific. But it feels right."

He once pulled a muscle in his back, and refused to take ibuprofen.
Said he didn't want to "baby it."

Classic MFDS.

Symptoms Include:

- Views all illness and injury as optional
- Refers to modern medicine as "soft"
- Frequently says:
    - "It's all in your head."
    - "You don't need a doctor. You need discipline."
    - "Sickness is simply a weak mind."
- Feels threatened by:
    - Therapy
    - Rest
    - Thermometers

Derek once called the flu "a mindset issue."

Notable Incident:

When Derek had COVID, he didn't tell anyone.
He still went to work.
Still lifted weights.
Still claimed he was "just fighting off a little fatigue."

He lost his sense of taste, but said:

"It's actually helping me eat cleaner."

He posted an Instagram story from his garage gym captioned:

"Tested positive for excuses. Prescribed discipline."

Therapist's Interpretation:

Mental Fortitude Denial Syndrome is a defense mechanism born from generational pride, masculinity myths, and an obsession with being "tougher than the modern world."

MFDS patients equate struggle with character. To them:

- Pain is a test
- Help is a trap
- And hydration is for the emotionally unstable

They often live by the mantra: *"If I don't talk about it, it's not real."*

Treatment Plan:

1. **Feelings Fluency Exercises**
   Practice naming your feelings without using the word "fine."
2. **Pain Scale Literacy**
   Learn that "10" is not "whatever."
3. **Vulnerability Exposure Therapy**
   Admit to a minor ailment in public.
4. **Empathy Drills**
   When someone else is hurt, respond with something other than "You'll be alright."
5. **Therapy Phrase of the Week**

   "Toughness isn't denying pain. It's doing what healing requires."

Self-Assessment: MFDS

"You don't need a nap. You need grit."

1. You're injured. You:
A. Rest and recover
B. See a doctor
C. Google it while mocking Google
D. Walk it off until you collapse or heal

2. You hear someone is in therapy. You think:
A. Good for them
B. Everyone should be
C. That's not for me
D. I have a garage and a punching bag

3. Your go-to solution for sickness is:
A. Fluids and rest
B. Medication
C. Ignoring it
D. Rage-lifting

4. Your spouse/partner has said:
A. "You need to rest."
B. "Please see a doctor."
C. "You're not fine."
D. "I can't watch you limp around like this anymore."

Mostly C's or D's?
You've got MFDS.
Your immune system is not impressed.
Your body is not a battlefield.
Let it heal without shaming it.

Jamison Carrier

Doctor's Notes:

Derek now admits he "might have felt off" for
three consecutive weeks.

He wore a knee brace... under his pants... but
hey—he wore it.

He hasn't canceled a cold plunge yet.
But he no longer judges people who do.

We're calling that... internal progress.
Even if externally, he's still pretending he's fine.

Jamison Carrier

PART IV: Career & Corporate Chaos

Where Everyone's a Brand and No One's Okay

,

Chapter Sixteen

Occupational Identity Broadcasting Syndrome (OIBS)

"How do you know someone's a nurse, firefighter, or pilot? Don't worry. They'll tell you."

Patient: Jake T.
Age: 38
Occupation: Pilot / Badge Wearer / Conversation Hijacker
Referral Source: His neighbor, who just wanted to borrow a ladder and ended up hearing about flight school

Session Notes:

Jake introduced himself like this:

"Hey, I'm Jake. I fly commercial."

He was not asked.

He then launched into a detailed story about turbulence, FAA regulations, and how "people just don't get how much responsibility we carry up there."

The conversation was about backyard mulch.

Jamison Carrier

Symptoms Include:

- Finds ways to insert their profession into any conversation
- Wears profession identity gear outside of work hours
- Has said:
    - "It's not just a job—it's who I am."
    - "There's just something different about us."
    - "You wouldn't understand unless you've done it."
- Uses professional jargon while ordering coffee

Jake once told a barista:

"Roger that, initiating double espresso taxi."

She responded:

"That'll be $4.75."

Notable Incident:

At a block party, Jake was asked, "So what do you do?"

Thirty-two minutes later, he was drawing diagrams in mustard on a paper plate to explain crosswind landings.

A child nearby whispered:

"Is he okay?"

Jake replied:

"I'm a pilot. I don't panic."

Therapist's Interpretation:

OIBS is not about pride in work.
It's about **merging identity with occupation** to
feel valuable and validated.

These individuals fear being *nobody* outside of
their role.
So they *become* their role.
Loudly.

The job isn't what they do.
It's who they are.
And they will remind you.
Every time.

Treatment Plan:

1. **Profession-Free Introductions**
   Practice saying your name without your
   title.
2. **Two-Topic Buffer Rule**
   Wait at least two unrelated topics before
   bringing up work.
3. **Jargon Detox**
   Replace industry lingo with normal human
   words.
4. **Off-Shift Identity Practice**
   Spend a full weekend not talking about
   your job.
   Jake called this "terrifying."

5. **Therapy Phrase of the Week**

> "My profession is part of me. It is
> not all of me."

Self-Assessment: OIBS

*"Let me know if I haven't mentioned my job in the last 10
seconds."*

1. You're meeting someone new. You say:
A. "Hi, I'm [Name]."
B. "Hi, I'm [Name], I work in…"
C. "Hi, I'm [Name], I'm a firefighter."
D. "Hi, I'm [Name]. Not all heroes wear capes."

2. Your wardrobe includes:
A. Whatever's clean
B. Subtle nods to work
C. Fifteen company-branded polos
D. A sweatshirt that says "NURSE LIFE "

3. You've described your work as:
A. A job
B. A calling
C. A way of life
D. "The front lines of the real world"

4. Your spouse has said:
A. "You work hard."
B. "You're passionate."
C. "Can we talk about *anything* else?"
D. "You told the Uber driver your full résumé."

Mostly C's or D's?
You've got OIBS.

You're not just your badge, your scrubs, or your flight log.

You're a whole person.
Even when you're off the clock.

Doctor's Notes:

Jake is learning to separate identity from occupation.
He introduced himself at a dinner party without mentioning his job.

Progress lasted 22 minutes.
Then someone asked about vacation travel.

He stood up and said:

"Actually, that reminds me—"

We'll get there.
At cruising altitude.

Chapter Seventeen

Professional Bio Distortion Complex (PBDC)

"You 'led a team'? You mean you opened once at Panera."

Patient: Taylor A.
Age: 22
Occupation: Resume Architect / Buzzword Curator / LinkedIn Novelist
Referral Source: A recruiter, who read her profile, called for an interview, and discovered she was "Director of Culture" at a hair salon.

Session Notes:

Taylor brought a printed copy of her resume to the session.

It included:

- "Strategic Operations Specialist" (she ran the cash register)
- "Brand Development Liaison" (she once helped design a new uniform shirt)
- "Client Experience Architect" (she offered punch cards)

She said:

"I just translate my value into professional language."

When asked if she's ever exaggerated, she said:

"I prefer to call it aspirational accuracy."

Symptoms Include:

- Inflates job titles to sound executive-adjacent
- Uses terms like:
    - "Thought leader"
    - "Global perspective"
    - "Human-centric optimization strategist"
- Has a LinkedIn profile that requires scrolling
- Posts long captions that start with:
    - "I don't usually post like this, but…"
    - "After much reflection…"
    - "Sometimes leadership looks like wiping down a table at 9pm…"

Taylor once described herself as a "solutions evangelist."
She was selling sneakers at the mall.

Notable Incident:

Taylor applied for a senior operations role at a tech firm.

Her cover letter said:

"As the former VP of Guest Flow and Rapid Deployment at a high-volume service brand, I

109

thrive in dynamic, customer-focused environments."

She was referring to her time serving in a Chick-fil-A drive-thru.

She added:

"We moved cars like Amazon moves packages. But with more grace."

She was not hired.
But her post about the experience got 118 likes and 12 "so proud of you" comments.

Therapist's Interpretation:

Professional Bio Distortion Complex is a self-worth camouflage technique.
The patient believes *reality* won't be impressive enough—so it's spun, elevated, and keyword-optimized.

The goal isn't deception.
It's recognition.

The resume isn't a document.
It's a mood board for who they wish they were.

They're not lying.
They're just focused on creative writing.

Treatment Plan:

1. **The Honest Title Challenge**
   List your last three jobs using the actual title and what you actually did
2. **Buzzword Reduction Protocol**
   Remove one jargon word per week (Starting with "visionary")
3. **Substance Over Spin Drill**
   Instead of writing about what your job *meant*, describe what you *did*
4. **Imposter Syndrome Flip**
   Remember: Real confidence isn't loud— it's accurate
5. **Therapy Phrase of the Week**

> "I can be honest about my experience and still be proud of it."

Self-Assessment: PBDC

"If I rewrite it with bullet points, it's real."

1. You describe your retail job as:
A. Sales associate
B. Customer service
C. Guest experience strategist
D. Brand liaison for consumer engagement

2. Your LinkedIn headline says:
A. Job title
B. Creative twist
C. "Connector | Storyteller | Culture Architect"
D. "Changing the world, one latte at a time"

3. You once:
A. Told the truth

111

B. Padded a detail
C. Wrote a cover letter longer than your college thesis
D. Used the phrase "empowered humans to connect with purpose"

4. A former coworker reads your profile and says:
A. "That's accurate"
B. "That's a stretch"
C. "Wait... were we at the same job?"
D. "You made that sound way cooler than it was."

Mostly C's or D's?
You may have PBDC.
You don't need a fancier title.
You just need to believe that what you actually did... matters.

Doctor's Notes:

Taylor removed "Transformation Lead" from her resume.
She now says "shift manager."
And you know what?

It still sounds impressive.
Because she was good at it.

That's real leadership.
No buzzwords required.

Chapter Eighteen

Reply-All Rage Disorder (RARD)

"One more 'Thanks!!' and I'm quitting my job."

Patient: Tanya R.
Age: 40
Occupation: Mid-Level Manager / Email Sniper / Silent Screamer
Referral Source: Her therapist, after Tanya threw her mouse across the room over a reply-all birthday chain

Session Notes:

Tanya entered the session tense, clutching her laptop like a hostage negotiator.

She opened with:

"I swear, if Gary from accounting says 'Happy workiversary!' to the whole company one more time…"

Earlier that week, she received an all-staff email about a potluck.

Sixteen people replied with:

- "Sounds great!"
- "Can't wait!!"
- "I'll bring something keto!"

By the eighth reply, Tanya muttered:

"I hope you all forget your forks."

Classic RARD.

Symptoms Include:

- Sudden rage at emails not directed to them
- Deep, irrational hatred of cheerful punctuation (especially "!!")
- Knows exactly who the serial reply-all offenders are
- Has considered creating a second inbox just to feel peace

Tanya once received an email titled "Important: System Downtime."
The first five replies were jokes.

She physically flinched.

Notable Incident:

A department-wide congratulations email went out for a coworker's promotion.

Twenty-seven people replied:

"Well deserved!!"
"So happy for you!"
"Couldn't happen to a better person!"

Tanya replied:

Jamison Carrier

"Please remove me from this chain."

Then immediately regretted being "that person."
But only a little.

Therapist's Interpretation:

Reply-All Rage Disorder is a workplace-specific
emotional dysregulation syndrome caused by
digital overstimulation, social obligation fatigue,
and inbox claustrophobia.

RARD sufferers don't hate kindness.
They hate *redundant broadcasted kindness*—especially
when it keeps them from real work... or
pretending to do it.

Every unnecessary reply-all is perceived as a
personal attack on their time, attention, and
sanity.

Treatment Plan:

1. **Inbox Filtering Protocol**
   Create smart folders to automatically sort
   chaos from relevance
2. **Breathe Before You Block**
   Pause three seconds before replying with
   "REMOVE ME FROM THIS CHAIN"
3. **The Reply-None Challenge**
   Go one week without replying to a single
   all-staff message
4. **Journaling for Judgmental Thoughts**
   Write down every snarky internal
   comment.

Do not send it. Do not Slack it. Just…
write.

5. **Therapy Phrase of the Week**

"I am not my inbox. I am not my
inbox. I am not my inbox."

Self-Assessment: RARD

"You're clogging my soul with your exclamation points."

**1. You receive a "Congrats!" email chain.
You:**
A. Reply with a kind message
B. Say nothing
C. Whisper "stop it" under your breath
D. Consider sending a virus through the reply-all
chain

**2. You once got 32 replies to an email. Your
reaction was:**
A. Joy
B. Annoyance
C. White-hot fury
D. You left work early to scream into a forest

**3. Someone says "Just replying all so
everyone's in the loop!" You say:**
A. "Good thinking"
B. "Smart"
C. "That loop is now a noose"
D. Nothing. But you unfollow them on LinkedIn

**4. Your email signature should probably
include:**
A. Your name and title

Jamison Carrier

B. Contact info
C. "Please don't reply all"
D. "Unsubscribe from humanity"

Mostly C's or D's?
You may have RARD.
It's okay.
You don't hate your coworkers.
You just want peace… and an "Only Reply to
Me" button.

Doctor's Notes:

Tanya now deletes reply-all threads before
opening them.

She's also learned to breathe deeply when
someone uses "team!" in an email subject line.

We're cautiously optimistic.
Unless someone forwards her a GIF of dancing
cats with the subject line "Happy Fri-yay!!"
Then all bets are off.

Chapter Nineteen

Hyper-Observational Correction Complex (HOCC)

"You can't not fix things. Even passive-aggressively."

Patient: Nicole L.
Age: 42
Occupation: Professional Detail Noticer /
Interior Grammar Designer
Referral Source: Her coworker, after Nicole
corrected her pronunciation of "charcuterie"
during a baby shower toast

Session Notes:

Nicole arrived on time.
Too on time.

She rearranged the throw pillows in the waiting
room.
Straightened a crooked frame.
And wiped a smudge off the door with her sleeve.

She greeted me with:

"Your shirt's untucked. But it works. Casual-
professional is hard."

She didn't mean it maliciously.
She meant it help-like.

Symptoms Include:

- Cannot ignore:
    - Grammar errors
    - Crooked signage
    - Misused idioms
- "Helps" people mid-sentence
- Rearranges silverware at restaurants "so it's even"
- Has said:
    - "Just trying to help!"
    - "You'll thank me later."
    - "It's pronounced 'espresso'"

Nicole once corrected the hymn lyrics on a church projector... during the service.
She walked to the booth and whispered, "It's 'angel' not 'angle'"

She says it haunts her.

Notable Incident:

Nicole was invited to a friend's new home.
Within 12 minutes, she had:

- Straightened a rug
- Commented on the kitchen lighting
- Moved a plant two feet to the left
- Said, "Oh, your kitchen outlets aren't GFC? Just something to keep an eye on."

She thought she was being helpful.
The friend thought she was *doing a free audit.*

Jamison Carrier

Therapist's Interpretation:

HOCC is an anxiety-rooted control reflex
disguised as "constructive input."

These patients are not trying to be critical.
They are trying to **restore order to the universe.**
One misspelled restaurant sign and off-center
picture frame at a time.

Correction is not meanness.
It is their love language.
With a minor in unrequested editing.

Treatment Plan:

1. **The Let-It-Go Challenge**
   Identify one thing per day you notice…
   and say *nothing*.
2. **Pause Before Helping**
   Ask: "Does this help them or just calm
   me down?"
3. **The Appreciation Swap**
   When tempted to correct, offer a
   compliment instead.
   (She tried. She complimented my…
   paperclips.)
4. **The Control Detox**
   Spend time in a slightly messy room.
   Breathe. Do not fix.
   Repeat until eye twitch subsides.
5. **Therapy Phrase of the Week**

   "I don't have to fix everything. I
   can notice… and let it be."

Self-Assessment: HOCC

"You're welcome. No one asked, but you're welcome."

1. You walk into someone's house and notice:
A. Their smile
B. Their vibe
C. Their crooked clock
D. Their clock, their dusty baseboards, and the
weird placement of the TV

2. You read a sign with a spelling error. You:
A. Ignore it
B. Laugh

C. Take a photo and send it to someone
D. Take a Sharpie out of your purse and fix it

3. A coworker misuses "literally." You:
A. Let it slide
B. Cringe silently
C. Whisper "figuratively" under your breath
D. Write a Slack message with definitions

4. Your spouse has said:
A. "Thanks for the reminder"
B. "You notice everything"
C. "Can you just *let me* do it?"
D. "You exhaust me. But the room does look better."

Mostly C's or D's?
You might have HOCC.
It's okay.
Your heart's in the right place.
Even if that frame isn't.

Doctor's Notes:

Nicole let someone say "expresso" in a conversation and didn't correct them.

She developed a headache.
But she survived.

She's now embracing what we call "graceful imperfection."

And no longer brings her level to dinner parties.

Chapter Twenty

Chronic One-Upper Syndrome (COUS)

"Oh, you did something cool? They've done it better. In Europe. Twice."

Patient: Brad M.
Age: 39
Occupation: Competitive Conversationalist / Humblebrag Technician
Referral Source: His pickleball partner, who said, "His toast at my wedding was about him."

Session Notes:

Brad arrived late.
He explained,

"Sorry, traffic was insane—but not as bad as L.A. during the marathon I ran back in 2016."

No one had mentioned traffic.
Or L.A.
Or marathons.

He sipped coffee and muttered,

"This reminds me of the espresso I had in Florence. Not quite the same, but it's fine."

He once heard someone had surgery and immediately responded,

"I've actually had two, but I recovered a lot quicker than expected."

Classic COUS.

Symptoms Include:

- Cannot let someone else have a moment
- Responds to good news with slightly better news
- Mentally translates every story into a competitive event
- Has said:
  - "Oh wow, *we* did something similar—except ours had more altitude."
  - "That's awesome! When *I* did that…"
  - "Not to brag, but…"

Brad once one-upped a child who lost a tooth.
Told him about the time he had six wisdom teeth removed and only took ibuprofen.
The child cried.
Brad said,

"He'll thank me someday."

Notable Incident:

At a wedding, the groom gave a toast about proposing on a mountain hike.
Brad followed it with:

Jamison Carrier

"That reminds me of when I proposed—sunrise balloon ride in Napa. Did it in French. Didn't even plan it. Just... felt right."

The groom has not spoken to him since.
Brad insists he was "adding color."

Therapist's Interpretation:

Chronic One-Upper Syndrome is an insecurity-masking mechanism disguised as enthusiasm.

COUS patients don't mean to steal thunder. They just can't bear to feel irrelevant.

They believe value is earned through comparison—so they compare compulsively.
If you climbed a mountain, they helicoptered over it.
If you got a promotion, they turned one down "because it wasn't aligned."

Their identity is stitched together with "me too, but better."

Treatment Plan:

1. **The Listening Exercise**
   Respond to stories with *questions*, not upgrades.
2. **The Silent Victory Rule**
   Think of your own story—then say nothing. Just nod.
3. **Celebrate Without Conversion**
   Practice saying, "That's awesome!" and leaving it there.

4. **Perspective Journaling**
   Each night, write about someone else's
   success without comparing it to your own
5. **Therapy Phrase of the Week**

   "Their win isn't my loss. It's not a
   contest."

Self-Assessment: COUS

"I'm not competitive. I just always win at conversations."

1. A friend tells you they ran a 10K. You respond with:
A. "That's incredible!"
B. "I've been thinking about doing one."
C. "I did a half marathon last year."
D. "That's cute. I did a Tough Mudder in a blizzard."

2. Someone shows you their vacation photos. You think:
A. "I'm happy for them."
B. "I want to go there someday."
C. "Ours was more scenic."
D. "Did they even do the catamaran?"

3. A coworker shares their kid's science fair win. You say:
A. "That's so cool!"
B. "What was the project?"
C. "My son did one in fourth grade too. He placed second *at state*."
D. "Wait 'til they start robotics. That's where it gets serious."

4. Your spouse/partner has said:
A. "Thanks for listening."
B. "That was supportive."
C. "Can you just let me have this one?"
D. "It's not always about you, honey."

Mostly C's or D's?
You may have COUS.
And yes, someone else has it too.
But that doesn't mean you have to win.

Doctor's Notes:

Brad is learning to celebrate others without immediately referencing his own success.

He recently heard someone talk about climbing Kilimanjaro and only said,

"That's incredible."

Then he bit his tongue.
Hard.

We consider that *emotional altitude training.*
And it's working.

PART V: Sports Psychosis & Suburban Glory

"They're 8 years old. No, they're not going pro."

Chapter Twenty-One

Vicarious Athlete Syndrome (VAS)

"You peaked in high school. Now your kid has to avenge your JV career."

Patient: Greg T.
Age: 44
Occupation: Commercial Real Estate / Sideline Strategist / Former Regional MVP (Honorable Mention)
Referral Source: His 9-year-old's soccer coach, who said, *"It's like coaching two teams—one of kids, one of dads."*

Session Notes:

Greg wore a varsity jacket to his intake session.
From 1997.
He referred to it as "vintage."
He opened with,

"You know, I would've gone D1 if my knee hadn't gone out. Just bad timing."

He's said this phrase in three different sessions.
We've stopped responding.

Greg recently got into a shouting match with a referee at a 4th grade basketball game.
Final score: 12–9.

Jamison Carrier

He posted a slow-motion clip of his son's layup with the caption:

"He's built different."

Classic VAS.

Symptoms Include:

- Wears branded team apparel with their kid's name on the back
- Speaks in second person about youth games:
  - "We've got playoffs next week"
  - "We didn't come to play"
  - "We're grinding this season"
- Has compared a 10U soccer ref to a war criminal
- Talks about their child's sport as though it's the draft combine

Greg once told another dad,

"I just want him to have the opportunities I didn't."
His son is in third grade.

Notable Incident:

Greg set up a 3-camera film review session after his daughter's 7U softball tournament.
Included commentary.
Used a teleprompter.
Sent the Dropbox link to grandparents.
No one opened it.

He also bought a GoPro for his son's flag football helmet.
The child quit midseason to take a pottery class.

Greg called it a "personal betrayal."

Therapist's Interpretation:

Vicarious Athlete Syndrome is a common generational performance disorder rooted in unresolved ambition, athletic nostalgia, and slightly too much creatine in the late '90s.

VAS patients don't want to control their kids.
They want **a redo.**
A second shot.
A chance to see their last name on a jersey that means something.

They're not trying to pressure.
They're trying to prove.

Treatment Plan:

1. **The "Not We" Challenge**
   Replace "we" with "he/she/they" for an entire week.
   (Greg said this "felt like betrayal.")
2. **Highlight Reel Fast**
   No posting slow-motion videos of children under 10.
   Especially not with dramatic music.
3. **Past Glory Quarantine**
   No references to personal sports

achievements for 14 days.
Not even "all-county honorable mention."
4. **Therapy Phrase of the Week**

"Their game is not my redemption."

Self-Assessment: VAS

"I'm just here to support—while screaming from the sidelines."

1. Your child scores. You:
A. Clap politely
B. Cheer and celebrate
C. Say "That's what we've been working on!"
D. Rip off your jacket and shout, "LET'S GOOOO!"

2. You describe your kid's sport using:
A. Basic facts
B. Light enthusiasm
C. Full playbook terminology
D. "They're getting looks from a couple travel teams"

3. Your gym bag still contains:
A. Resistance bands
B. Protein powder
C. Cleats (just in case)
D. A whistle and laminated plays

4. Your child has said:
A. "Thanks for coming to the game."
B. "You cheer loud."
C. "Can you not yell at the ref?"
D. "I want to quit."

Mostly C's or D's?
You might have VAS.
You're not a bad parent.
You're just running a full offense from the
bleachers.

Doctor's Notes:

Greg is learning to sit during games.
He claps quietly now.
And only shouts instructions if the ref is out of
earshot.

His son still plays flag football.
But they compromised—Greg's GoPro now films
Greg on the sidelines instead.

We call it "game tape for personal growth."

Chapter Twenty-Two

Armchair Ref Rage Disorder (ARRD)

"You saw the whole play from 83 feet away. The umpire? Too close to see what happened."

Patient: Dennis W.
Age: 52
Occupation: Regional Sales Manager / Official Watchdog / Voice of Justice from the Bleachers
Referral Source: A Little League umpire who finally said, "You need more help than I can give you."

Session Notes:

Dennis showed up wearing wraparound sunglasses on top of his head and a polo with his kid's baseball team embroidered on the chest.

Before sitting down, he asked if we validate parking.
Then muttered,

"Be nice if someone *officiated* that."

He refers to every youth official as "Blue," regardless of the sport or shirt color.
He once called a 13-year-old line judge at a volleyball match "a disgrace to the game."

Classic ARRD.

Symptoms Include:

- Yells "Come on, Blue!" at inopportune times
- Believes "they're out to get us" is a valid explanation for a bad call
- Thinks slow-motion replays should be mandatory at middle school games
- Has memorized the rulebook but never read a parenting book

Dennis was once asked to leave a 6th grade basketball game after shouting,

"That's a travel! This is BASIC STUFF."

The player was his nephew.
He was doing his best.

Notable Incident:

Dennis was nearly banned from a community softball league after standing behind home plate with an airhorn to "help the ump stay focused."

His wife sat ten rows away.

After a questionable strike zone at a 9U tournament, Dennis confronted the ump postgame with a printed screenshot from a livestream.
He highlighted the pitch location.
With a ruler.

Therapist's Interpretation:

Armchair Ref Rage Disorder is a control-adjacent outburst condition triggered by perceived injustice, mild nostalgia, and suppressed competitiveness.

ARRD patients often believe they're protecting the integrity of the game.
But in reality, they're projecting unresolved control issues onto anyone with a whistle.

The louder they yell, the more they believe they're contributing.
They confuse intensity with advocacy.
And think *"Let the kids play"* means *"Let me scream louder."*

Treatment Plan:

1. **Whistle Awareness Exercise**
   Count to five before reacting to a call.
   (Dennis said five seconds is "how long it takes to lose a championship.")
2. **Referee Empathy Training**
   Volunteer to officiate one game.
   Any age. Any sport. Preferably preschool soccer.
3. **Reframe the Game Protocol**
   Instead of questioning every call, cheer every hustle play.
   (Even the other team's. Deep breath.)
4. **Therapy Phrase of the Week**

"My job is to cheer, not to
challenge the officiating
hierarchy."

Self-Assessment: ARRD

*"I'm not yelling. I'm just passionately clarifying from 100
feet away."*

1. A ref makes a questionable call. You:
A. Shrug it off
B. Groan internally
C. Shout "COME ON, BLUE!"
D. Bring out a laser pointer and a copy of the
rulebook

2. You describe youth sports officiating as:
A. A thankless job
B. Imperfect but necessary
C. "An absolute joke"
D. "Corrupt, biased, and probably rigged"

3. After a game, your kid says:
A. "That was fun."
B. "Tough loss."
C. "That ump hates us."
D. "Please stop yelling during my games."

4. Your spouse has said:
A. "You're passionate."
B. "You get a little worked up."
C. "I'm sitting with the other parents today."
D. "You're why there's a sign about yelling at
refs."

Jamison Carrier

Mostly C's or D's?
You might have ARRD.
It's okay.
We know you care.
But the ump doesn't need a co-pilot with a
Gatorade bottle and a Bluetooth headset.

Doctor's Notes:

Dennis has agreed to watch one game per week
without commenting on calls.
He's learning to say things like "Good hustle" and
"Nice effort."

He did yell once last week—but it was "Great job,
ref."

We're calling that progress.
And nobody got ejected.

Chapter Twenty-Three

Team Identification Delusion (TID)

"We need the win this week." Sir, you sell insurance.

Patient: Bryce K.
Age: 36
Occupation: Insurance Agent / Armchair Coordinator / Merchandising Machine
Referral Source: His wife, after he referred to the Dallas Cowboys as "us" and then ghosted a friend for being an Eagles fan.

Session Notes:

Bryce arrived in full team gear.
Hat. Hoodie. Slides.
Even his Yeti tumbler had a decal.

He opened the session with,

"Sorry I'm a little down… tough loss yesterday."

He did not play in the game.
He did not attend the game.
He did not have a friend or family member in the game.

He *did* post a 4-paragraph Instagram story about it, including the phrase:

"We just didn't want it bad enough."

Classic TID.

Symptoms Include:

- Uses "we" when referencing pro sports teams
- Takes rivalries personally
- Believes playoff outcomes affect personal productivity
- Schedules fall weekends around the team's bye week

Bryce once texted his pastor mid-sermon:

"Wrap it up—kickoff in 8."

He has a fantasy team.
He refers to it as "his boys."
He's benched most of them.

Notable Incident:

Bryce once flew to Buffalo in January to "be there for the team."
He didn't have a ticket.
He stood in the parking lot wearing a sleeveless jersey and a beanie.
Got frostbite.
Said it was worth it.

He also once referred to a rookie QB as "my guy" after watching two highlight reels on YouTube.
The rookie was later traded.
Bryce said he felt "betrayed."

Jamison Carrier

Therapist's Interpretation:

Team Identification Delusion is a parasocial loyalty disorder characterized by deep emotional investment in a team of strangers.

TID patients find identity, community, and purpose through fandom—but blur the lines between spectator and stakeholder.

They don't just support.
They internalize.
They *belong*.

Wins are euphoric.
Losses are personal.
Trades are heartbreaks.

They know every stat—except their spouse's birthday.

Treatment Plan:

1. **The "Not Us" Rule**
   Replace "we" with the actual team name.
   (Bryce tried. He said now he was the betrayer.)
2. **Post-Game Reflection Protocol**
   One sentence max.
   No Instagram essays.
   No videos filmed from the couch with sad piano music.
3. **Stat-Free Weekend Challenge**
   Take one weekend off from obsessing over scores.

Go outside. Touch grass. Talk to a human.

4. **Therapy Phrase of the Week**

    "I am a fan. Not a free agent."

Self-Assessment: TID

"They didn't play well, and I haven't either."

1. Your team loses. You:
A. Say "Tough game" and move on
B. Vent in a group chat
C. Refuse to speak for the rest of the night
D. Unfriend someone who rooted for the other team

2. You've said "we" in reference to:
A. Your family
B. Your coworkers
C. A college or professional sports team
D. All of the above—especially the team

3. A rival fan talks trash. You feel:
A. Amused
B. Mildly annoyed
C. Personally attacked
D. The urge to key their car (but don't… probably)

4. You've missed a major life event because of:
A. Travel delays
B. Illness
C. Work
D. A 1:00 p.m. kickoff

147

Jamison Carrier

Mostly C's or D's?
You may have TID.
The team appreciates your loyalty.
But you're not on the payroll.
And your kids miss you during games.

Doctor's Notes:

Bryce is now practicing healthy detachment.
He still wears team gear, but no longer refers to
roster changes as "betrayals."

He recently said,

"Tough loss. They'll bounce back."

They. Not *we*.

We cried.
Together.

Chapter Twenty-Four

Fantasy Football Identity Crisis (FFIC)

"You lost sleep over a tight end who doesn't know you exist."

Patient: Josh R.
Age: 33
Occupation: Software Developer / Fantasy GM / Human Sleeper Pick
Referral Source: His boss, after Josh called in "emotionally unavailable" on Monday because his kicker missed a 37-yarder.

Session Notes:

Josh entered the session holding an iPad and muttering about red zone efficiency.

He apologized for being late.

"Waivers opened at noon. I had to make moves."

He referred to himself as "QB-deep but RB-thin." When I asked what that meant in life terms, he said,

"Exactly."

Classic FFIC.

Symptoms Include:

- Talks about his fantasy team like it's a small business
- Yells at NFL players on TV as if they can hear him
- Has a group chat named "The League" with a custom logo
- Refers to real-life injuries as "inconvenient"
- Says things like:
  - "I should've started him."
  - "That cost me the week."
  - "He was questionable, but I believed in him."

Josh once benched a player out of spite.
The player scored 27 points.
Josh said he was devastated.

Notable Incident:

Josh drafted during his anniversary dinner.
Mid-toast, he screamed,

"Let's goooooo!"
He got Chris Olave in the 5th round.

His wife ordered dessert alone.
They're still married.
Barely.

He once lost a game by 0.12 points.
He cried in the shower.
Then made a meme about it.

Jamison Carrier

Therapist's Interpretation:

Fantasy Football Identity Crisis is a behaviorally immersive simulation disorder where imaginary stakes feel painfully real.

FFIC patients experience inflated highs and catastrophic lows based on the performance of professional athletes they've never met, but feel personally connected to.

It's not a game.
It's *emotional stock trading*.
And every Monday morning is judgment day.

Treatment Plan:

1. **Boundary Reintroduction Protocol**
   Say out loud: "I do not manage a real team."
   Repeat until the blood pressure drops.
2. **Emotional Diversification**
   Find at least one hobby not tied to stat projections.
   (Pickleball is acceptable. Obsessing over it is not.)
3. **Trade Talk Reduction**
   Limit fantasy football conversations to 15 minutes per day.
   Group chat memes do not count.
4. **Therapy Phrase of the Week**

   "My value does not depend on a fantasy player's performance."

Self-Assessment: FFIC

"I care more about this fake league than my real job."

1. A player gets injured. Your first thought is:
A. "That's terrible, hope he's okay."
B. "Man, that stinks for his team."
C. "HOW COULD HE DO THIS TO ME?"
D. "My season's over. I'm cursed."

2. Your family plans a weekend trip. You say:
A. "Sounds great!"
B. "Let me check my schedule."
C. "Can we do Red Zone on the road?"
D. "I can't. It's rivalry week."

3. You've yelled at a player through your TV because:
A. They made a mistake
B. You were frustrated
C. You needed 6 more points
D. You're "just asking for effort"

4. You've described fantasy football as:
A. A fun hobby
B. A weekly ritual
C. A lifestyle
D. "Therapy, but competitive"

Mostly C's or D's?
You might have FFIC.
And while your fantasy team deserves respect...
so does your actual life.

Jamison Carrier

Doctor's Notes:

Josh is now setting lineup reminders that don't
interfere with social events.
He recently watched an NFL game without a
single fantasy player involved.

He said it was "weirdly peaceful."
Then immediately added another league.

Progress is relative.
So are fantasy points.

Syndromedy

Jamison Carrier

Bonus Chapter: Technological Mismatch Disorder

They changed the Wi-Fi name and now I can't watch church

Chapter 25

Technological Mismatch Disorder (TMD)

"They changed the Wi-Fi name and now I can't watch church."

Patient: Harold B.
Age: 68
Occupation: Retired Postmaster / Accidental Hacker / Proud Owner of Three iPads
Referral Source: His daughter, after he called her crying because "the TV said no signal and I haven't even touched anything!"

Session Notes:

Harold arrived with a legal pad full of handwritten questions.
Labeled: *"Computer Stuff To Ask That Man."*

He started with:

"What exactly is Bluetooth? Do I need it?"

Then added:

"I think my email got unplugged."

Jamison Carrier

He owns a smartphone but still prints directions from MapQuest.

Classic TMD.

Symptoms Include:

- Ends every text with their name, like it's a telegram

   "See you Thursday. Love, Dad"

- Refers to Zoom as "The Zoom"
- Asks "Can they see me?" every 90 seconds during video calls
- Forwards jokes from 2009 with subject lines like "Fwd: Fwd: Fwd: THIS IS TOO FUNNY!!!!"

Harold once watched a YouTube ad and thought it was the actual video.
He shared it and commented, "This guy really knows what he's talking about."

It was for carpet cleaner.

Notable Incident:

Harold accidentally replied-all to a church leadership email chain with a chain message titled:

"FW: If You Love Jesus, You'll Send This to 10 People Right Now"

He also replied:

"Nice to see everyone's names. How is Pastor's dog doing?"

He has no idea it went to 47 people.

Therapist's Interpretation:

Technological Mismatch Disorder isn't about intelligence.
It's about **interface trauma.**

TMD patients were raised in a world of knobs, buttons, and yellow legal pads.
Now they live in a world where "tap and hold" means different things on every device.

They're not resisting change.
They're just navigating a touchscreen world with calloused hands and dial-up instincts.

Treatment Plan:

1. **Two-Device Max**
   Harold currently owns three iPads, two remotes, and one universal control no one understands. We're downsizing.
2. **The "Don't Touch It" Principle**
   If it works, leave it alone. (He has already violated this five times.)
3. **One Platform Mastery**
   Choose one: Email, text, or FaceTime. Master it. Then—*maybe*—add another.
4. **Digital Grandkid Mentorship Program**
   Grandchildren act as patient tech support, paid in hugs and soft peppermints

5. **Therapy Phrase of the Week**

> "I don't have to understand the
> Cloud. I just have to not delete the
> internet."

Self-Assessment: TMD

"I don't trust that thing. It listens to me."

1. You've tried to search for something online by:

A. Typing keywords

B. Asking your phone politely

C. Saying "www dot" out loud

D. Posting the question on Facebook and hoping your niece answers

2. You've experienced tech failure. Your first response is:

A. Restart the device

B. Check YouTube

C. Blame Wi-Fi

D. Unplug it and pray

3. Your favorite button is:

A. Back

B. Home

C. The one that closes everything

D. "Print"

4. Your signature tech move is:

A. Screenshots

B. Bookmarking

C. Printing emails

D. Holding your phone up and asking, "Is this on?"

Mostly C's or D's?

You may have TMD.
But don't worry.
You are **not alone.**
Unless you turned on airplane mode and can't turn it off again.

Doctor's Notes:

Harold has officially stopped forwarding fake IRS warnings.
He has a written list of passwords, kept in a folder labeled "Passwords."
He now signs off video calls with confidence and only *sometimes* stays on by accident.

We call that progress.
And Harold calls it "good enough."

Jamison Carrier

Final Chapter: Yes, It's a Thing.

The closing message of Syndromedy

Yes, you have a syndrome.
You just haven't been diagnosed yet.

That's the beauty of being human—we're all
carrying quirks, contradictions, and low-grade
behavioral chaos. Some of us spiral in group texts.
Others require a checklist to feel joy. And a few
of us (you know who you are) cannot find the
Ranch dressing even if it's glowing.

But that's not brokenness. That's human.
It's funny.
It's familiar.
It's shared.

Syndromedy isn't about judgment. It's about
recognition.
It's about finally naming what makes us weird—
and laughing about it together.

You don't need to fix every flaw.
You just need a good diagnosis and some people
who get the joke.

So, on behalf of Dr. Sy Camore and the
unlicensed, emotionally exhausted field of fake
behavioral science:

You're not broken.
You're just funny.
And definitely diagnosable.

Syndromedy

Jamison Carrier

A Note From the Author

In Case You Thought This Was Just About Laughing

When you're growing up, you just assume you're normal.
Your routines. Your family. Your quirks. They're all you've ever known.
But as you get older, and meet more people, and see more of the world, you start to realize…
Some of the things you and your family do are, well—*weird*.

You may have noticed a certain obsession with maximizing time in these pages. That's not satire. That's me. I once scheduled bathroom breaks on vacation. Kathy still hasn't forgiven me

At first, our differences are funny. Then it's awkward.
And, it can become isolating.

Because if we're not careful, our differences—our settings, our rhythms, our emotional wiring—can create distance. We pull away. We misunderstand. We judge.
All because someone else's version of normal doesn't match ours.

But what if we turned that around?

What if we made room for the fact that everyone has a syndrome or two?
What if we laughed *with* people instead of at them?

What if we focused less on what separates us, and more on the beautiful mess we all share?

My family—*my tribe*, as I call them—is like most. We've had seasons of incredible joy and big wins. And we've faced deep loss, too—more than our share.
We've lost people we love far too soon.
We've wrestled through relational messiness, incurable illness, and the kind of pain that doesn't fit neatly in a social post.
But through it all, we've stayed connected. We've showed up. We've laughed, cried, argued, and diagnosed each other mercilessly.
Because that's what family does.

We may disagree—*strongly, loudly, and occasionally with pie charts*—but we love each other. We've got each other's backs.
And I'm learning to extend that same kind of grace to people *outside* the tribe.

No, we're not inviting everyone over to Sycamore Shores. (That's sacred ground.)
But I want to be the kind of person who is kind to everyone, curious about their story, and always down to share a laugh—even if we're wildly different.

So whatever quirks you carry, whatever dysfunction you bring to the table, just know:

You're not broken.
You're just funny.
And definitely diagnosable.

Jamison Carrier
And you know what else?

You're a winner.
You've got what it takes.
And I'm glad you showed up.

Jamison Carrier

About the Author

Real Jamison. No clipboard.

Jamison Carrier is not a licensed therapist, but he's been observing human behavior for decades—from boardrooms to barn lots, dealership showrooms to late-night group texts. He's a speaker, entrepreneur, creative connector, and the founder of Relentless Dealer Services. He built a career by helping leaders grow and businesses scale—while quietly cataloging the quirks that make us all wonderfully dysfunctional.

Jamison is a grateful member of what he lovingly calls **The Tribe**—a family known for its love, loyalty, and a strong genetic predisposition toward mockery, group project chaos, and deeply mismanaged calendars.

When he's not writing, speaking, or diagnosing strangers under his alter ego, **Dr. Sy Camore**, you can find him spending time with his wife Kathy, investing in people, attempting to find something (that's right in front of him), making a checkmark on his to-do list, running, cycling, or sitting by the lake at **Sycamore Shores**—his home and personal retreat, shared with family, friends, and the occasional bear rug.

This is his first book.
Unless you count the three he's been "about to finish" since 2009.

Syndromedy

Jamison Carrier

Co-Conspirators

Because none of this dysfunction happened in isolation.

First, I want to thank **God**—because clearly, He has a sense of humor. I mean... just look at us. If nothing else, *Syndromedy* is proof that grace covers not just sin, but also *calendar spiraling, reply-all rage, and inability to find the Ranch dressing.*

To **Kathy**—my partner in life, my best friend, and the most beautiful soul I know. You've walked with me through everything, supported dreams that sometimes sounded more like jokes, and brought three incredible people into my life the day we married. You were a single mom—strong, steady, and full of grace. I'm forever grateful that you brought **Tori, Trisha, and Joey** with you. They are mine too—by heart, by choice, and by the grace of God. I'm grateful to be part of their story. You complete me. And also, you're the only person Dr. Sy Camore won't attempt to diagnose--at least not out loud.

To **The Tribe**—you know who you are. Thank you for the laughter, the chaos, the loyalty, and the countless moments we probably should've written down... and now we have. I love you all. We are weird, but we're weird *together*.

To my **parents**—the best you'll find anywhere. You modeled love, faith, sacrifice, and the power of showing up. Also, let's be honest: you played no small role in shaping a fully diagnosable family tree. And I wouldn't change a thing.

To Dom —You've been more than a partner in business; you've been a brother, a steady presence, and the kind of friend who shows up no matter what's going on. You carried the weight during seasons when I couldn't, and never once asked for credit. You believed in the mission, in the work, and in me.

Also... your self-diagnosed misophonia may have quietly inspired this entire book. So really, this is all your fault. Thanks, and sorry.

To Amy—Thank you for writing the foreword and giving this book the right kind of heartbeat. Even though you're technically a figment of my imagination, you understand people deeply. Your words helped this whole thing land softer, funnier, and truer than it would've without you.

To **Joey**—we miss you every day. Your life continues to impact others, and your story drives so much of the love behind this project. Grief can pull us inward, but love always pulls us outward. This book is part of my own fight to keep loving, keep connecting, and keep laughing—*not to avoid the pain, but to walk through it with purpose.*

I once asked a *real* therapist for a solution to keep me from becoming bitter.
I said, "Put it on the whiteboard."
He laughed. Then he drew a scale.
He told me: *"Hate isn't the opposite of love. Apathy is. If you love, you act. As long as you keep loving and serving others... you won't become bitter."*

He was right.

Jamison Carrier

That's part of what drives *Syndromedy*.
Loving people enough to laugh with them.
Seeing quirks not as flaws—but as fingerprints.

So here's to the weird, the wounded, and the ones
still showing up.
You're not broken.
You're just funny.
And definitely diagnosable.